Lydia and Joachim F. Richter — BRU DOLLS

Lydia and Joachim F. Richter

BRU DOLLS

Hobby House Press

Published by

Cumberland, Maryland 21502

Top to Bottom:
Illustration on Page 2:
Leon Casimir Bru - marked: "BRU J^{NE} 8" - Portrait
Illustration on Page 6:
Circle Dot Bru - a boy dressed in very elegant clothes -
suit made from cream-colored silk and richly embroidered with pearls.

We would like to give our thanks to all of the following people who were extremely helpful in providing us with informative material, documents, as well as the loan of dolls so that this book could be published.

Alfred Barsotti, Ursula Brecht, Zelda H. Cushner, Ursula Gauder-Bonnet, Kath Engels (Doll & Toy-Museum Rothenburg on the Tauber), Doris Giebelhausen, Christiane Gräfnitz, Ella Hass, Jane Kingdon, Wiebke Kramer, Margie Landolt, Alfred Mignon, M. Alain Renard T, Sabine Riecken, Hannelore Schenkelberger, Karin Schmelcher, Elke Schuldt, Carol Ann Stanton, Mrs. Steiner (Doll Museum, Stein-Am-Rhein), François Theimer, Matthias Wanke (Limburg-Lahn) T, Charlotte Wolff.

The illustrations of the patent drawings on pages 8-13 were gratefully made available to us by François Theimer, Paris.

Text and Editorial Cooperation: Karin Schmelcher

Publishers: Lydia and Joachim F. Richter

Conception and Layout: Joachim F. Richter

Photographs: Alfred Barsotti: pages 19, 24-27, 40, 41, 55, 62, 63, 68, 69, 74, 80-83, 88, 92, 93, 99(4x); Ursula Brecht: pages 2, 22, 23, 42, 48-51, 53, 59, 65, 67, 75, 99(2x); Kath Engels pages 96 above left; Joachim Giebelhausen: pages 58, 85; Christiane Gräfnitz: pages 20, 38, 60, 84, 86, 87, 89; Ella Hass: pages 90, 91, 99(1x); Jane Kingdon: pages 34, 38; Wiebke Kramer: page 96 above right; Margie Londolt: pages 28, 52, 54; Richard Merrill: page 98; Alfred Mignon: pages 29-31, 33, 99(1x); Lydia Richter: pages 57, 64, 94, 97; Joachim F. Richter: pages 18 above, 96 above middle; Hannelore Schenkelberger: pages 6, 18, 44-47, 66; Karin Schmelcher: pages 56, 70-73, 76-79, 95, 99(1x), 101; Elke Schuldt: page 100; Charlotte Wolff: pages 36, 37.

Body Sketches: pages 12, 13, 16, 17, 21, 35: Karin Schmelcher

Translation: Michael T. Robertson

ISBN: 0-87588-357-5

Table of Contents

The "High Praise" of Bru Dolls

At the latest, with the birth of the Bébé Bru, the auspicious hour of the highly cultivated porcelain head doll struck. As, like the Circle Dot Bru, whose vision of a charming, chubby and intimately loved child became reality, was the BRU J^{NE} the ideal doll creation bordering on perfection of a beautiful young girl. That is why collectors of these dolls look so transfigured and are fascinated by their charm. Similar to that of a harpist who helps us escape the daily chores with his music, so does the grace and charm of these dolls keep us enraptured. Even those who are not doll lovers or collectors view Bru dolls with respect, let themselves be captured by the radiance and often cannot put their minds at rest, that these creations, which stand in front of them are not living children, but dolls. Everyone who can see and feel is penetrated with the charm of these human-like images made by the hands of artists. They are perfected through lovely paperweight eyes, beautifully shaped hands, feet and body, and through stylish clothing, which reflects the art of French fashion. In a double sense, Bru dolls become an experience and a precious belonging.

The hunting fever of passionate collectors seems to have no limits; often great sacrifices are made so that a Bru doll can be taken home. Impatience, occasionally unreasonableness, euphoria and enthusiasm come hand-in-hand. Yes, the spectrum of emotional feelings reaches from shouting to the skies with delight to a deathly grievance and does not stop for fanaticism. The desire in wanting, which is engraved at childhood, is now newly awakened in Bru fans and vibrates more strongly than ever on the nerves of enthusiastic collectors. Bru lovers know what they talk about and also know what they do when they sell some of their doll collection so that they may be able to buy only one favorite from this money, which hears to the magical name of Bru. To combine these beautiful dolls, which are unattainable for many, in a representable book of facts and illustrations so that collectors and dealers can be supplied with helpful information was the main irresistible concern of author and publishers. So we, as the first publishing house, managed, like in 1982 on the occasion when the book about Käthe Kruse dolls was published, to present a book on this special topic. This makes us very happy and proud. Also, patent drawings and the description of different types of bodies give the Bru enthusiasts first-hand information which up till now has never been brought to light.

Although we have, over many years, published a lot of successful doll books, no one has succeeded, either in German speaking countries or abroad, in producing a fundamental and extensive book about the well-beloved and at the same time rare Bru dolls. A difficult, but interesting challenge! Without the unselfish and helpful cooperation of favorably inclined collectors, without the photographs and other documentational material entrusted to us and without the intensive research, as well as editorial cooperation from Karin Schmelcher, the realization of this book would never have been possible. Therefore, we would like to thank everyone who has been helpful and generous. This circle of people stretches from Germany across other European countries and as far as the United States of America!

We wish you much happiness in the study of this book.

Joachim F. Richter

The History of the House of Bru

Patents and Doll Types

The history of the House of Bru cannot be seen isolated from the overall development of the French doll industry in the 19th century. The company was founded in a period of a general industrial boom, especially the doll industry, and it found itself from the very start surrounded by strong competition like Jumeau, Huret or Steiner, all of whom had been successful for some time. The producers competed with inventions and new developments so that they could continue to exist in this expanding market. The perfection of the dolls in their anatomy, the improvement in the articulation of the limbs, as well as the mobility of the head and eyes all stimulated their ingenuity. New production methods and materials were used, for example gutta-percha, which for the last two decades was the favorite material of Huret. Bru started experimenting with it later. All new developments and inventions were registered as patents (Brevet), which, by paying an appropriate tax, were protected for five, ten or fifteen years. These patents, supplied with descriptions and working drawings, are today an important source for collectors in classifying and dating their beloved and often very valuable dolls.

The founding of the House of Bru fell in the middle of a period of a great boom, circa 1867; the exact date of the founding of the company is impossible to establish. The company existed, however, with certainty in 1867, since Leon Casimir Bru, the founder, had registered in that year his very first patent. 1867 was the year of the World's Fair in Paris where Mlle. Calixte Huret had her biggest success and was showered with praises and awards. It also was the "Golden Age" of the *Poupée Parisienne*, a lady doll or fashion doll." Mind you, in France if one talked about a "poupée," one meant a doll with an anatomy of a grown-up woman! In those days the ideal beauty had a narrow waist and a well-developed breast and hip region. The standard norm of its proportions was 1:7, meaning the overall height of the body corresponded to seven times the length of the head. It seems important to us for the dating of French dolls, especially those of the House of Bru, that the beloved "Bébé" of today at that time did not exist. At that time, if one mentioned Bébé dolls, one meant those coming from England, like the expensive wax dolls or the bébé in the style of Japanese dolls, often referred to as the "Motschmann-type." The Bébé Bru in those days hardly existed, nor did the Bébé Steiner or the Bébé Jumeau.

Leon Casimir Bru started his career with the type of doll which at that time was fashionable — the lady doll. At first the body was completely made of leather and the breastplate and head of bisque, most likely produced by Gaultier, from whom most doll manufacturers of that time obtained their heads. The patent of 1867 describes such a lady doll with a screaming mechanism (criante-screaming) placed in the thorax. It was a simple rubber ball which, when pressed, activated the voice mechanism. In an aesthetic sense this invention was questionable. Can one imagine a well-dressed lady letting out a scream similar to that of a squeaking rubber animal? This patent, at the same time, shows the preference of Leon Casimir Bru for rubber materials.

In that same year, Leon Casimir Bru presented another patent, his *Poupée Surprise* (surprise = surprise). This two-faced doll head was attached at the center to wooden rod and showed, when turned at the axis, a laughing and a weeping face, without the wig being moved. The head could be moved manually or later with a built-in turning mechanism, which was activated by a button. The physiognomy and the material for the head were optional. In fact, there were dolls that existed with a laughing and crying face and with a wakeful or sleeping face. Naturally, these

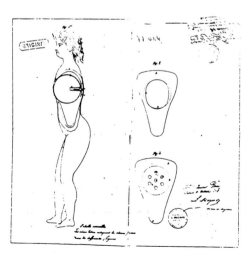

A new technique of a screaming (crying) doll.

technical frivolities found great interest, especially with grown-ups, but for the further development of the doll they were without any meaning. There was a difference in the case of the patent from February 5, 1869, whereby it deals, like Bru wrote, with "...the perfection in the production of dolls, using rubber in the production of the body..." In the drawing enclosed with the patent application one

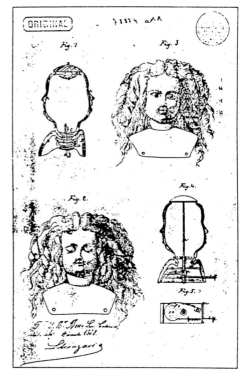

Patent drawing of a two-faced doll with an open-eye and a closed-eye doll.

Left: Side view of a patent drawing of a surprise doll, Poupée Surprise, with a smiling and crying face.

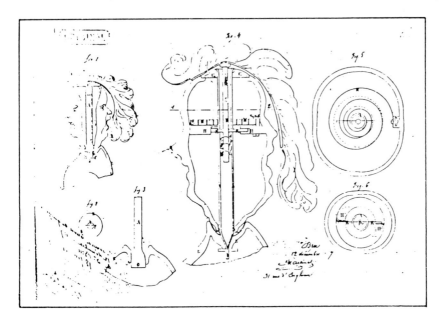

recognizes the technical and formal perfection of a jointed body of a lady doll with joints even at the waist and at the ankles. This wonderful body, which allowed a maximum of mobility, was produced before and continued to be made out of wood; this meant a great deal of work and, therefore, was expensive. If one succeeded to pour these bodies in molds, then this was a great progress in reducing the production costs. According to the demands and the funds available, the Bru company in 1869 could offer the lady doll in the following models:

1. Complete leather body, including the arms and hands
2. Leather body, jointed arms and hands made of wood or hard rubber
3. Body fully jointed, made of wood or hard rubber, or even gutta-percha.

As a head model, one finds mostly a face with an indication of a smile. That is why collectors also call this doll "Mona Lisa." This head can be referred to as the typical Bru lady head. Only a few of these specimens were marked, if one disregards the letter on the shoulder plate, which was a size marking. Later, the lady dolls produced under Chevrot were marked, of course, on the breastplate "B. J^NE et Cie."

In an advertisement from 1870, the Bru company wrote the following about their products and it seems important to us to quote this, since this script was at the same time a type of summary about Leon Casimir Bru's work. He died during the war in 1870: "...dolls with unremoveable and removeable clothing, traditional and the most newest models, doll heads of all kinds, specialty of new-style dolls, revolutionary new and exclusive in their style, made from hard-rubber, gutta-percha and carved wood, fully jointed, even at the waist, on the feet and hands, which provided the doll with a certain special gracefulness; soft-rubber dolls, dolls with two faces, especially fine-leather dolls with jointed arms and hands."

Patent drawing of a Bru jointed body made of wood.

After the death of Leon Casimir Bru and until his son, Casimir Bru (Bru Jeune), became of age to take charge of the company, Mrs. Appolene Bru managed the company. In May 1872, she registered a patent under her own name. It dealt with the insertion of a musical box into the inside of a conventional doll.

One can be sure that Casimir Bru, Jr., felt from early on at home in the company of his father and that he spent his time in the company until he could take over the business. The inheritance that his father left him was interesting and quite versatile. Besides the production of dolls, he obviously was fascinated with the production of hard and soft rubber. This fact is hardly known among doll collectors; the production of these things took a large place in the company's manufacturing. In September 1875 Casimir Bru, Jr., registered a skull as a trademark (Marque deposée) and in an advertisement of 1876 he wrote: "…inventor and producer of rubber-animals as joke-articles and for surprises, like for example rats, lizzards, fishes, bats, toads etc. … All of our models are registered goods, others are also patented. To avoid any possible mistakes, they require our trademark, which is depicted by a skull…"

The latter proves that other companies were also occupied in the production of rubber toys and that the competition here was also great. Bru also mentions that the factory for these toys was in Menilmontant but the sales address was 226 Rue Saint Denis, Paris. Around 1870, in the realm of doll production, a small revolution was starting, which at the time Casimir Bru took over the company was slowly, and in the late 1870s developing even faster: the birth of the "bébé." At the beginning of the 1870s still in the experimental stage, the Steiner company (1873), manufactured the first bébé. Emile Jumeau recognized rather early the potential of this new type of doll and in 1875 also brought out a bébé on the market. In a very short time he brought it to perfection, thanks to his modern production methods, so that he even won a gold medal (Medaille d'or) for it at the World's Fair of 1878. The success of the bébé did not go unnoticed by Casimir Bru; however, he could not decide to produce ball-jointed bodies out of papier-mâché. Instead, he decided to make the bébé with a leather body. This bébé had, in contrast to the poupée, childlike proportions. His proportions were 1:5, that meant the body length amounted to five times the head length (without the neck). Otherwise, the construction of the bébé was very similar to that of the poupée, the only difference being that the forearms and hands were made of bisque. The body of the bébé still had a waist and altogether was rather immobile. The face had childlike features with chubby cheeks — the collector knows this doll by the name of "Bébé Breveté" (the patented bébé).

The disadvantages of this bébé with a leather body are quite obvious when compared with the ball-jointed bodies of the competitors. First of all, there is the unstableness, as well as its immobility. Also, the leather body was not very robust. The seams could burst and the contents would then fall out. The advantages were mainly found in the aesthetic area. All visible parts of the doll, like the head, breastplate, forearms and hands were made of bisque and therefore modeled more delicately and naturalistically than was possible with the composition bodies. Casimir Bru tried to make a compromise. He improved the leather body by making a simple cut, which had a more childlike form. The waist was left out, the body became more compact and it was stuffed with lighter materials, namely cork shavings and horsehair, instead of the heavier sawdust. At the same time, the breastplate was enlarged and was designed more realistically with modeled small breasts. Above all things, his new bébé received a head which surpassed everything with its childlike radiance, compared to what the competitors had to offer. It is the head of the Circle Dot Bru, named after the frequently found marking, a dot and circle on the back of the head, often combined with a B on the forehead. It is this chubby face with its sweet turned-up nose and its slightly open mouth with

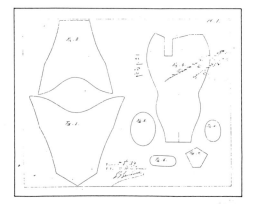

A detailed drawing of a body for the Bébé Bru.

modeled-on tip of a tongue or teeth, which depicted so perfectly a small child and delights collectors from all nations. At the beginning, it received several small changes but in the following years, the Circle Dot Bru became the typical Bébé Bru and stood in competition to the Bébé Jumeau, Bébé Steiner, Bébé Schmitt and many others, who had almost exclusively ball-jointed bodies. The disadvantages of the leather body were quite obvious. The main advantage was the low cost of production, which played a major role in the fierce competition.

About the same time, Casimir Bru also offered a luxury doll, his Bébé Modèle, a joint-body doll, which technically and in form was copied from the wonderful jointed body of the lady doll, however, with childlike proportions, without the joint at the waist, but with joints on the hands and at the ankles. This doll, with a body carved completely from wood, represented a small masterpiece and could not be compared with the up till then known French bébés. The price of this doll must have been much higher than that of other dolls, which explains the relative rareness of this model. This doll was also produced completely from gutta-percha, including the head, but this material proved to be rather undurable, explaining why Bru dolls made from gutta-percha are very rare today.

In the same year, October 3, 1879, Bru patented an invention which was to prove to be a great "winner" for the company — the "Bébé Téteur." Its success was so long-lived that this bébé was still being produced in the 20th century by S.F.B.J.; the body was the only thing changed. The Bébé Téteur was a doll-child, which when supplied with a bottle, could drink, a very impressive effect, based on a simple physical principal. In the inside of the head there was a pear-shaped rubber ball whose opening ended at the open mouth of the doll. A bottle filled with water, mixed with a few drops of Eau de Cologne which produced the milky color, was connected by a tube to the rubber ball inside the open mouth. Through an opening at the back of the head, one could depress the rubber ball and by letting go, a suction was produced which emptied the contents of the bottle into the rubber ball — the doll was drinking (téter = sucking). By repressing this ball, the fluid returned back into the bottle. This mechanism was improved in 1882; a metal hoop or ring was built in and by turning a butterfly screw located at the back of the head, the necessary pressure on the rubber ball was achieved. It is a great pity that today this mechanism does not function because the rubber has since grown brittle. The earlier Bébé Téteurs have a leather body of the Circle Dot Bru, from 1883 onwards they had the so-called "Chevrot body" and around 1890 onwards they had a jointed body made either of wood or composition. The later models from the S.F.B.J. period could even be found to have a S.F.B.J. Jumeau body, a fact which caused collectors not to buy them and made them think that these had been manipulated with. However, the earlier models of the Bébé Téteur are the more valuable ones.

In 1882 Casimir Bru introduced another "child wonder," the "Bébé le Gourmand" (gourmand = sweet-toothed, voracious; the first word is meant here). This doll could be fed by placing small morsels of food into its mouth. A movable tongue transported the food into the head and the morsels would fall through a hollow space down into the legs, where an opening in the sole of the foot was found. A flap connected to this opening was opened and the morsels of food could be removed. A child could demonstrate to her unknowing girlfriend that the doll could actually "eat and digest," like an advertisement claimed. For the doll to be able to do this, the legs from the knee downwards had to be made of bisque, wonderful and realistically shaped child's legs, a very special and valued detail among Bru collectors. Furthermore, the Bébé le Gourmand had a leather body of the Circle Dot Bru. The weakness of this doll is immediately seen and it concerns mainly the hygienic aspects. What happens when over a long period of time the contents were forgotten

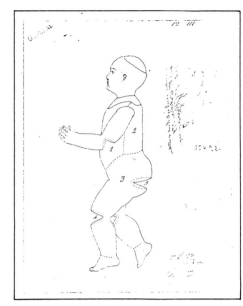

A complete drawing of the body of the Bébé Bru.

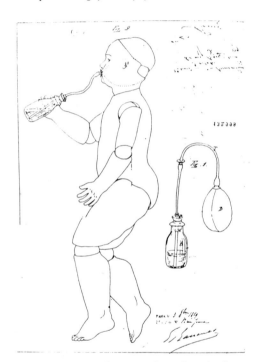

Patent drawing of the Bébé Téteur with a mechanical sucking device, which today, however, hardly functions because the rubber has decomposed. The head was mounted on a composition body made by Steiner.

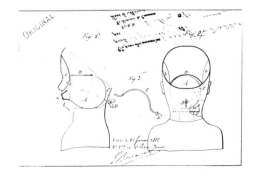

Patent drawing of the oldest Bébé Téteur, whose sucking device compared with the second version was not mechanical, but instead, functioned by manually turning a butterfly screw situated at the back of the neck.

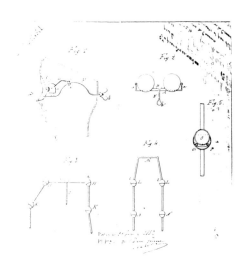

The movable eyelids, arms and fingers were to be protected by this patent, whose joints were the so-called "universal joints."

The darkened surfaces in the drawing illustrate which parts of the body were made of leather.

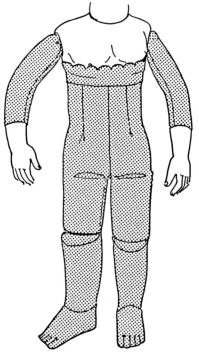

The new leather body with childlike rounded proportions. Breastplate with lightly modeled breasts.

to be emptied out or even worse when the doll mother, with lack of understanding, feeds her doll with soft food which blocks the mechanism? An explanation for the rareness of doll may be found here.

In the same year, 1882, Casimir Bru applied for another patent, a further step to perfecting and imitating realistic movements. He also at one time invented an eye mechanism where the eyelids closed over the stationary eyeballs. Until then there was only one mechanism where the eyeballs themselves were the only thing that moved. On the same patent drawing one can also recognize a system for universal joints which served to give better articulation to doll bodies and to allow the doll all kinds of possible movements; even the fingers had these joints. Both inventions show clearly the tendencies of Bru, Jr., towards perfection, which meant at the same time that the spectrum of doll types was becoming more variable and that the production of these dolls was becoming far more complicated. Without a doubt, the ingenuity of Bru had contributed a lot towards the further development of the doll. Is impossible to tell if this was profitable for him. The scarcity of the dolls with the above mentioned technical details leads us to believe the opposite.

Since a portrayal of the company's history of the House of Bru did not exist or happened to have been lost, there will always be questions which will remain unanswered. For example, why did Casimir Bru, Jr., after a few years, give up the control of his father's company. The reason may lie in the versatility of his interests. As we have seen, the doll production was only one branch of the House of Bru. New materials like rubber and gutta-percha interested him very much, maybe more than the production of dolls. He was a man full of inventiveness and he saw that there was a limit set with creating dolls. In the same year, 1883, not long before the Bru company was sold, he acquired a patent under the name of Bru and Jeannin (not: Jumeau, like it was often written; see *Polichinelle*, No. 22) for an object which had nothing to do with the Bru doll. He wrote that it was a kind of "mechanical revolving machine" (a kind of merry-go-round?), which he called "Flotille Internationale" and that it was meant for annual fairs. Maybe that was the reason why he sold the branch of the company that produced dolls so that he could devote more time to these things. The new owner, Henri Chevrot, let the doll production run further under its successful name.

Nothing is exactly known about Henri Chevrot's origin, nor about his background. One can assume that he came from the same line of business. Under his control the company learns the needed concentration for one type of doll, the Bébé Bru. The first thing it received was a new body. On November 23, 1883, Chevrot submitted a patent for this body, which was considered to be the classical Bru body, coveted and admired by collectors today. It especially differed from the previous bodies through its mobility. The bisque forearms were not rigid, but were connected to the upper arm with a joint. The upper arm, just like the thighs, consisted of metal casings which were covered with kidskin. The lower leg of this new model was made of wood and was very well formed, whereby the toes especially were surprisingly detailed. The lower legs were also connected by joints to the thighs. The Bébé Bru could at last stand, sit or kneel without any problems. Sometimes the lower arms of the so-called "Chevrot body" were made of wood instead of bisque. They were less elegant, but not as breakable. This variation has confused some collectors.

Not only did the new body become more mobile, but also the proportions had changed. The extreme waist was very striking because according to the dominant fashion at that period, even small children had this desired waist, which was supported accordingly with a corset.

Together with the less chubby-cheeked face marked "BRU J^NE" and size number, the Chevrot Bru embodied, contrary to the Circle Dot Bru, an already grown-up girl. The breastplate still showed the modeled breasts, however, less accentuated. With larger models, the hinted shoulder blades are very noticeable. This Bébé Bru, together with the extremely extravagant and always the latest fashionable clothing, represented a small masterpiece, and today one is not at all surprised that Chevrot won several gold medals with this doll.

From the old models Chevrot only took over the Bébé Téteur, which then received the Chevrot body; the Bébé le Gourmand, at least at the beginning (but later on it is not mentioned in his advertisements) and the Bébé le Dormeur (dormeur = sleeper), which received the eye mechanism. These three doll types

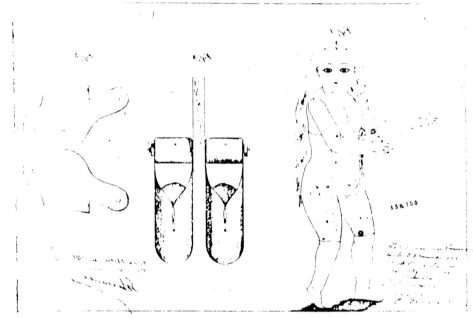

A detailed drawing of the joint connections which were used from 1884 onwards.

together with the new Bébé Bru Jne were highly praised by Chevrot in an advertisement in *Bottin* from 1884. The lady doll was not mentioned anymore but certainly it was still being produced. It had become less and less fashionable. The address of the House of Bru was given as 1 et 3 Boulevard de Strasbourg (on the corner of Bd. St. Denis).

The Bébé Bru of the Chevrot era was without a doubt a very successful doll. The many well-kept examples prove this. However, Bru never produced the large numbers that their largest competitor, Emile Jumeau, did. Jumeau had a very modern expanding factory in Montreuil-Sous-Bois in which his bébés were produced under his own management, from the top of the hair right down to the soles of the shoes.

This was somewhat different with Bru. His salesrooms and workshop on the Boulevard de Strasbourg did not offer enough space, mainly not for a factory, which it was written that the heads were being made in Montreuil-Sous-Bois, but whether it dealt with Bru's own porcelain factory remains unclear. A porcelain factory requires a very large investment and also many years of experience in dealing with this material. One suspects that parts of the doll were produced on order, like for example the metal parts of the body.

An advertisement on the occasion of the Paris World's Fair of 1889 gives information about the palet of the offers of that time of the company: "...gold medals in Paris, Barcelona and Melbourne. 25 inventions patented (not all of them concerning the Bru Dolls). Large factory of dressed and undressed Bébés. New unbreakable Bébés made from hollowed out wood, solid and lighter than those made from cardboard. Unbreakable heads (the latest novelty) of mixed mass, so beautifully modelled and painted like a bisque head. The Bébé Brus are the only ones, who have natural eyelashes. They differ due to their graceful hands and feet, as well

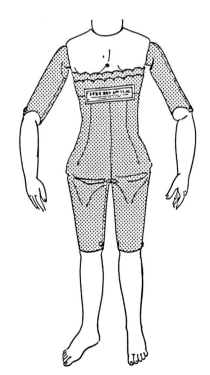

A tailored leather body of the so-called Chevrot Bru, whose forearms were made of bisque and the legs of wood.

as through their beauty and their tasteful clothing. Bébés Téteurs, patented s.g.d.g, delightful Bébés, who can drink by themselves. Bébés made of hard-rubber, guaranteed to be unbreakable. A factory for women, men and children's heads made of bisque for ready-made clothiers, hairdressers, shops for undergarments, hat makers and draper's shops etc., half as expensive as wax heads."

This advertisement contains an important piece of information about the production of heads — a question which has still not been clarified about who actually produced these heads for the Bru dolls. Bru, that means Henri Chevrot, wrote here that he had a factory of women, men and children's heads made of bisque. If he had produced them, then consequently he made his own heads. In the short time of his management (1884-1889, five years), he could have hardly had the time and the energy to build-up such a factory. This allows for speculation that Henri Chevrot, before he bought the doll department of the Bru company, had owned a porcelain factory. Maybe he was the supplier for the BRU J^{NE} and because of this, they knew each other. Maybe this factory was in Montreuil-sous-Bois, where from 1883 onwards, like we have read, the heads of the Bru dolls were produced. This may be very plausible, a possibility which until this day has never been confirmed.

The competition among the French doll producers was very great and a few companies had to give up. At the end of the 1880s and especially in the 1890s, the pressure from the outside, here meaning the German doll industry, was becoming greater. Not only in France, but mainly on the international markets, the German competition was becoming a threat to one's own existence. They brought the French doll producers under a strong downward trend on prices and naturally, they tried to retaliate by producing even more cheaply. This meant that the luxury item of great quality of the past now became a doll of even poorer quality. Since there are dolls still in existence from this period, we can easily trace this fact. Inspite of all efforts, several companies perished. This development caused the remaining companies to join in a combined venture in 1899, under the name of S.F.B.J. (Société Française de Fabrication des Bébé et Jouets).

A Table on the Periodic Classification of Popular Bru Dolls

	1867	1870	1875	1876	1879	1880	1885	1890	1895	1899	1900
Fashion or Lady Dolls, also called "Mona Lisa"	├						┤				
Bébé Breveté				├		┤					
Circle Dot Bru					├		┤				
Bébé le Téteur					├						┤
BRU J^{ne}						├		┤			
BRU J^{ne} R								├		┤	

Notes on the above table: Like the title states, this table is only for assistance. It supplies a quick summary and does not raise any rights on entirety. For example, for comments on the "surprise" doll, one should refer to pages 8, 32 and 33 and with reference to "Bébé Petit Pas," as well as "Bébé Baiser," page 15. With regard to the Bru J^{ne}, one should refer to the main text, since under this name there is an earlier and a later version, different types of bodies, and so forth. Concerning the periodic demarcation, one should consider that with certain Bru types, a smooth transition was given. In 1899 the House of Bru entered the joint venture of the S.F.B.J.

In this period a new change occurred in the management; in 1890 Paul Girard became the new boss of the House of Bru. This new change was hardly surprising, if one knew that Girard was a relative of Casimir Bru. At the same time Casimir Bru opened up a new business not far away from the Bru-Girard Company. His factory was "Articles de Paris" (= Parisian Articles); at Porte Sainte Denis, 2 Boulevard Bonne-Nouvelle.

Paul Girard took over the company in a difficult period. He went to work with full vigor and like Casimir Bru — maybe he was influenced by him — he was full of new technical ideas and obtained six additional patents between 1891 and 1897.

Several of these are explained here. On September 23, 1891, the "Bébé Petit Pas" (small step) appeared, a doll with a built-in walking mechanism which could move its head and say "Mama" and "Papa." In 1892 he created a mechanical doll, a doll which could breathe, speak and sleep. Anyone who had seen or experienced this doll in action, how the chest rose and fell, will confirm that the sight of this was rather frightening. Like always, the frequency or scarcity of a doll will tell us whether the doll was successful or not in those days.

In May 1895, Girard applied for a patent of the "Bébé Baiser," a doll which had a pull hinge in the arm and when activated, could blow a kiss, and in 1897 he was able to realize a doll that could do everything at once: walk, blow kisses, speak and move its head.

All these efforts to remain competitive through technical frivolties cannot obscure the fact that the "Bébé Bru's" quality was declining. Later, examples with open mouths do not remind us at all of the former quality of the Bébé Bru and especially the Chevrot Bru.

In 1899 the House of Bru ceased to exist.

The Bébé Bru continued to be listed for some time by S.F.B.J., but this is not a subject of this book.

An advertisement of the House of Bru in a daily newspaper.

Bru Heads — "Thousand-and-One Faces"

If one talks with Bru collectors, the question often arises, which face does one prefer the most and which rare and especially expressive "mold" does one search for? Bru lovers always speak of the thousand-and-one different faces of the Bru dolls. For others the faces of Bru dolls are all alike. Which is correct?

Both questions are correct! First of all, like with other masks, one overlooks the so-called family likeness with Bru. "Typically Halbigish," say lovers of Simon & Halbig dolls. A trained eye will also recognize a Kestner or Jumeau without even looking for a neck mark. On the other hand, the "Bru" had so many different possible expressions that it could take one's breath away. She could be touchingly childish with a girl-like innocence, but also arrogantly stuck-up, "rebellious" as one collector said once, dreamy or wide-awake, secretive or with a questioning look. She could also be sulky (boudeuse). One could continue on forever to express further differences of expression.

Did Bru produce so many different head types? The answer is rather amazing! Leaving out the head of a lady doll and looking only at the Bébé Bru, we will find three basic models (physiognomy), which brings out this variety.

First of all there is the face of the Bébé Breveté, the earliest child head of Bru. It is a sweet round child's face with a somewhat heavier receding chin portion.

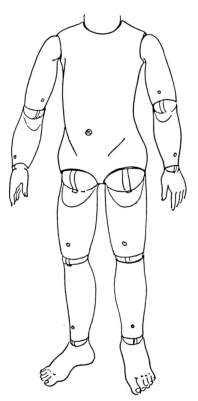

A *fully-jointed wooden doll body with childlike proportions (no wasp waist).*

After this comes the face of the Circle Dot Bru. It is even more childlike. The cheeks are distinctively chubby and heavy, as is typical for a well-nourished small child with milk teeth. The eyes of this doll compared with those of the Bébé Breveté are larger. Both dolls had this pronounced childlike innocence in common. However, the third face had the greater capability in changing its expression. It is the head of the Bru J^NE, a well-balanced girl's face with round but not chubby cheeks, a more prominent chin region and a well-formed nose. It is unbelievable that all the different Bru J^NE faces should come from the one and the same master mold — and yet it is true. If one looks at several Bru heads from the same perspective, from the front, side and profile and if one refrains from looking at the painting and the size of the eyes, one is basically dealing with always the same face. It is amazing what a difference the painting makes! Women especially know the small makeup tricks with which one can transform the eyes, lips and cheeks with different shades and how one can change one's looks using them. Whether the lips are fully painted-over and slightly beyond the shape of the lip edges or only thin and half-painted out makes a great difference. Also, the corners of the mouth give the face its character. If they are turned upwards, the doll smiles, turned down gives the effect that the doll is slightly pouting. The fact that the eye openings were cut out by hand has an additional significance. One does not have to explain that large eyes give the face a totally different expression than small or narrow eyes, not to speak of the color of the eyes as well.

The general coloring of the head was also a question of fashion. That is why earlier dolls were painted in a lighter and paler tone than later ones. The "elegant paleness" seems, at least with Bru, to have gone out of fashion around 1890; also a lady of the Parisian society could have stood model for the strongly accentuated eyebrows of the French bébés in a certain period. This was especially noticeable with Jumeau, but Bru did not remain spared from this unchildlike fashion.

The objection that there were also Bru heads with slightly open mouths and a molded tip of the tongue or even with open mouths has no essential meaning for the master mold. For an expert, it is relatively easy to transform or change the face from the original form. For better understanding, it is definitely helpful if one occupies oneself with the production of bisque heads (for example see *The Collector's Encyclopedia of Dolls*, pages 404-408) or one talks with modern doll makers who work with porcelain. Even the BRU J^NE R marked head comes from the master mold and the changes are recognizable. Between the lower lip and chin a triangular dimple was added and if the doll received an open mouth with teeth and sleep eyes, as was fashionable at the turn of the century, there was not much left in recognizing the earlier BRU J^NE head.

Bru With a Fully-articulated, Fully-jointed Wooden Body

This extremely mobile doll body was formally and technically copied from the lady doll made of wood; merely the proportions were childlike; the waist was left out. The joints were connected by wooden pegs so that no rubber bands or coils were needed inside the body. The possibilities of mobility were perfect and that is why it was superior to the ball-jointed bodies of the competitors. It is not marked.

The head of this body is an earlier BRU J^NE head and sometimes also the Circle Dot head; in very rare cases the head of the Bébé Breveté was used. The coloring is light and delicate.

The possible markings were (see mark at the left): This model was also available completely made out of gutta-percha. It was a pity that only a few of these examples have survived. This doll should not be mistaken for the much later Bru with a composition body and head. Regarding the so-called Chevrot Bru, please refer to page 61.

Bru With a Jointed Body

Towards the end of the 1880s, still under the management of Chevrot, the Bru company decided to also produce a joint body. It was first made from wood and composition and then from a completely "hollowed out" wood, which was lighter and more durable, like an advertisement from 1889 emphasized. This decision also had economic factors, since the Chevrot body was without a doubt expensive to produce.

There are several types of joint bodies but they all have the following characteristics in common: the body is of good quality, with perfect harmonious transition at the joints. It always had a waist; fingers and feet were carefully modeled. The differences were mainly found in the materials, as already mentioned, either of wood, composition or quite often from both. The transition models still had the bisque forearms of the Chevrot Bru. The hands connected to the forearms could either be articulated or were stationary. The position of the cut in the upper torso of dolls with a voice box was covered by the notched leather band of the Chevrot Bru; even the well-known sticker was not missing. The Bébé "Petit Pas" had a walking mechanism in the hip joint. It was also covered by leather. Only the very later models, like the bébé that could walk, speak, throw kisses and move its head, had simple but to a great extent very poor bodies. The jointed bodies of the Bébé Bru are marked on the back. Quite often this marking is missing. Therefore, it is important that one imprints this body formally in one's mind, which is not too difficult since the Bru body slightly differs from those of its competitors.

The head of the jointed Bru body was at the very beginning still identical to the head of the Chevrot body; both bodies were still being produced together. In the 1880s this head changed somewhat in the coloring and was always marked "BRU JNE." Most likely under the management of Girard (the exact date is unknown to us) did the markings change from "BRU JNE" into "Bru JNE R," but also into "BRU JNE R/Y.M." The presumption that Y.M. stood for YEUX MOBILES (mobile eyes) remains unconfirmed; many of these dolls with this marking also had fixed paperweight eyes. Minor changes, such as the dimpled chin, which became more accentuated, were mainly made to the heads by Girard; in addition there were such essential changes that one could speak of a new model head. Through changes in the painting, the open mouth with teeth and through sleep eyes, the old BRU JNE face can only be recognized by a very well-trained eye. Above all, the childlike softness is lost. Possible markings of the Bru with a jointed body are shown below; the numbers are size numbers and serve only as an example.

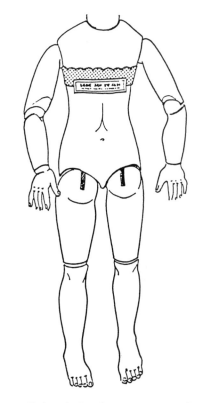

A jointed body made of wood, composition or a combination of both.

BRU·J^{NE}
6

BRU. J^{NE} R
10

BRU J^{NE} R
BREVETÉ S·G·D·G.
Y8M

An original Bru dress in very good condition.

The Size Classification in Numbers and Inches (cm) is Impossible

Different as compared with Jumeau, where the size numbers on the head (0-16) always corresponded to a certain overall size of the doll, this cannot be exactly done with Bru. If one were to compare ten different Chevrot Brus of the size 9 with each other, one would see that the overall size of the dolls vary approximately 4in (10cm) from one to another. Whereby those dolls, who were apparently manipulated, were unmarked.

A certain help is offered if one compares the head number and the number on the breastplate. As a rule, both numbers should correspond. However, often the company did not hold to this rule. There are Bru dolls which remained untouched and yet had different head and breastplate numbers. A sure eye for proportions can often help far more than depending on numbers. When the doll is undressed, one can see rather quickly whether the head and body fit together.

Bru Quality or Bru Ingenuity?

The so-called Bru quality is often major talk among collectors. This term is often deceiving, since it is often related by some to the special qualities of the head, especially to the bisque or coloring. With intensive inspection of a lot of Bru heads from the various eras, one comes to the conclusion that the Bru company carried out a rather lax quality control. A lot of "Brus" had unclean surfaces and enclosed air bubbles in the porcelain, as well as in the painting. Especially with eyelashes and eyebrows, one will find quite a few painting errors, like the paint running together in the eyelashes or thick and thin eyelash strokes next to each other. Furthermore, Chevrot Brus and also Girard Brus often have a rather strong complexion, which, was at the time, fashionable. Since one assumes that at least the earlier Bru heads were produced by Gaultier, it is rather odd that precisely this company was known to produce exceptionally high-quality heads. This fact, however, speaks more against Gaultier being the producer of Bru heads. Maybe collectors who, impressed with the term "Bru quality," may have thought more about the well-formed bisque hands, the perfectly modeled toes, the strong expressive face, the complete appearance of the doll or also the technical perfection of the Chevrot body. If one takes everything into account, then one should speak not of Bru quality, but more about the Bru ingenuity.

Dolls and Fashion

The strong social changes brought forth in France and elsewhere in Europe due to the growing industrialization of the last century had a certain effect on the fashion. For a long period of time, only the aristocracy and courtiers were responsible for fashion. As the wealth of the middle class grew, even a minimal affluence among the working class brought forth a buying class, who, carried by their new self-confidence, also wanted to be surrounded with luxuries.

This trend is especially seen in fashion; the addiction to show oneself and to keep up appearances becomes stronger, so that all levels of society are seized by this. Even the small factory worker or sales girl spends, naturally within the limits of her modest possibilities, everything, so that she can be dressed suitably for the Sunday stroll. Who could demonstrate the fashion better of this period than a "Parisian" with her trousseau? For a long time the earlier lady dolls were the ambassadors of the Parisian fashion. This changed completely with the rise of fashion prints or fashion magazines, and last but not least, through the appearance of the first mannequins in the

Circle Dot Bru as an elegant boy in an exquisite silk suit richly covered with lots of pearls. (Also see page 6.)

fashion scene and their significance towards the play doll. A doll, not in today's sense, but listening to the spirit of time, was more an object of representation or possibly had educational functions. In this period (1870-1880), a new model baby, the "bébé," appeared. It was only a play doll, but just like with children who were dressed up for show, these doll-children also had to be extravagantly dressed. Dolls of this era, which today have been kept in their original condition, demonstrate the ideal French bébé and show how luxurious doll clothing was. The most expensive materials such as satin, silk, velvet, lace and brocades were used; even furs or pearls were not dispensed with. The shoes were made from the finest leather or covered with satin, and even with the underwear up to and including bodices; nothing was left out. It was difficult for children's hands to dress these dolls, but practice with playful persistence and manual skill helped the small doll mother. Special magazines, i.e. *La Poupée Modèle*, were specifically devoted to the small girl, with patterns and fashion suggestions, or to understanding mothers, so that the doll was always dressed in the up-to-date fashion.

Since in every small child a small grown-up is predominantly seen, the fashion for children was copied from the grown-ups. Bodices for small children were not unusual, as well as all other undergarments (dessous) which a girl had to wear. Also, the outer garments were fashionable, except when they were rather restrictive and unpractical and, therefore, not fitting for a child. The narrow waist of a lady of society was also an example for young girls, however, less pronounced, but adapted to the childlike anatomy, more likely implied. The cut of the clothing was in any case tight fitting and at the end of the 1870s and through 1880s, it had a strong accentuation of the hip region, which one could call a "low waist." This region was emphasized using bows, frills and other applications, especially the back side, where the so-called "Tournure" of the ladies' fashion was also emphasized with girl's clothing.

What applied to small girls was a "must" for their dolls. At least the dolls could not complain about the lack of comfort. With the Bru doll, especially the Chevrot Bru, one could tell from the body its preference for closely fitting tailored clothing. The strong pronounced waist does not comply with that of a child's anatomy, but it is important for the fashionable clothing. The clothing of the BRU J^{NE} is always fashioned after this basic pattern. It is indifferent what kind of material is used and whether it was meant for summer or winter clothing, or clothing for daily wear or for special occasions. The dress in hanger form, a dress fitting for a child with shoulder pads and a wide flowing skirt, only became fashionable at the end of the last century.

The costs for doll clothing showed not only in the expensive material used, but also in the artistic workmanship of the fabrics and lace. The cut of the dress consisted of many components, which were pleated and ruffled, and a tendency to combine different fabrics applied next to each other was preferred. Velvet, especially dark red or blue, was combined with silk, either in the same color or a shade lighter. Laces and ribbons, mostly ecru-colored, were used frequently. Other favorite color combinations used were turquoise, light blue or pink combined with white or ecru trimmings. All of these luxurious materials and fabrics, which were used for the ladies' fashion and for which the French manufacturers were famous for (for example silk from Lyon), were also used for making doll clothes. The Bru company attached great importance to their fashionable outfits for their dolls. This was always stressed in their advertisements. It is obvious that hats and bonnets belonged to the outfits of a Bru doll and that the material used should match the dress, likewise with umbrellas and capes. Bru dolls wore shoes which were marked on the soles with "BRU," an ideal advertising space, especially when the doll was sitting.

An undergarment with lace borders and attractive red leather shoes of the Oriental Bru illustrated on pages 68 and 69.

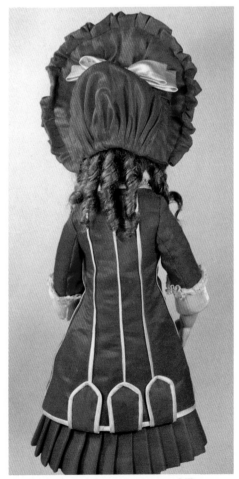

The back view of a very striking dress of BRU J^{NE} shown on pages 62 and 63.

Chapter 1

Bru Lady Dolls

Leon Casimir Bru marked "L." Socket head on a breastplate made of bisque.
Chevrot leather body with forearms and hands made of bisque, lower legs
and feet made of wood, 24in (61cm), - circa 1889.

The fashion or lady doll from Bru is often called "Mona Lisa" because the smiling face of this head, which is mainly found on different lady doll bodies, reminds one of the secret smile of this famous lady. Maybe there were other types of heads but this, however, was used for the Bru ladies. Apart from several stationary (fixed) shoulder heads which were attributed to Bru, this doll generally had a movable shoulder head mounted on a bisque breastplate. The head is normally unmarked, while the breastplate is often marked with one letter which denotes the size of the doll. The breastplate of the lady dolls from the Chevrot era are more accurately marked "B. J^{NE} et Cie."

The body came in three versions: the leather body, whose arms and legs were also made of leather, the leather body with jointed arms (see illustration at the bottom left-hand side) and the fully-jointed body made either from wood, hard rubber or qutta-percha (see illustration at the bottom right-hand side).

Dolls in their original boxes, whose lids had an illustration of one of the three types of doll bodies, helps with the identification of the Bru lady. A Bru lady doll with original clothing or even with a trousseau (completely equipped with different dresses, undergarments, bodices, hats, umbrellas, handbags, and so forth) is naturally far more valuable.

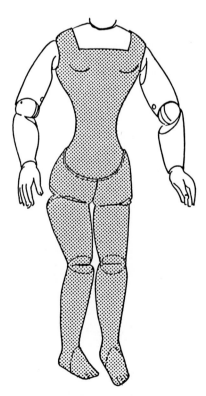

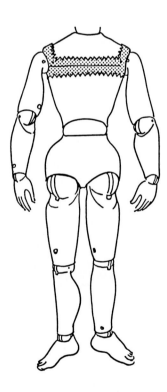

Left: A leather body with jointed arms. The shaded areas show those parts made of leather.

Right: A fully-jointed body made either of wood, hard rubber or gutta-percha.

Above and on page 23: Leon Casimir Bru marked "E," called either the "Smiling Bru" or "Mona Lisa." Socket head on a breastplate made of bisque fastened to the wooden body with leather bands, fixed (stationary) blue paperweight eyes, closed mouth, original wig, detailed wooden body with 13 joints (two shoulders, two elbows, two wrists, two thighs, two knees and two foot joints and one at the waist). Hands made of wood, 16in (41cm), circa 1875.

*Above and on page 25: Leon Casimir Bru unmarked fashion
doll. Socket head on a bisque breastplate fastened to the wooden
body with leather bands, gray-blue paperweight eyes, closed
mouth, detailed wooden body with 13 joints, one of which is
located at the waist, circa 1875.*

Leon Casimir Bru unmarked fashion doll. Socket head on a bisque breastplate, blue paperweight eyes, closed mouth, original mohair wig, leather body, forearms and hands made of bisque, old clothing made of cotton covered with flowers and lace trimmings, original shoes, approximately 18in (45cm), circa 1870.

Leather body of the doll illustrated on this page and page 27.

Leon Casimir Bru fashion doll marked "D." Socket head on a breastplate made of bisque, brown glass eyes, closed mouth, body, arms and hands made of leather, 15in (38cm), circa 1875.

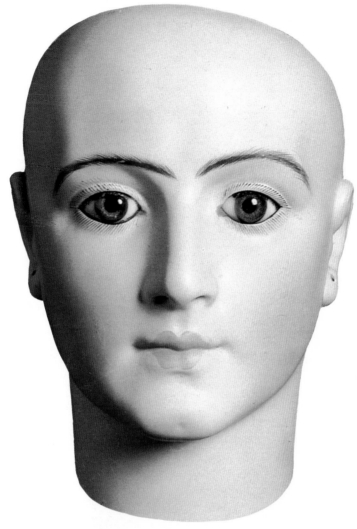

Bru doll head of a mannequin doll marked "B BRU Nº 3."
Stationary blue eyes, closed mouth, height of head 5½in
(14cm), from 1890.

Above and on page 31: Leon Casimir Bru marked "BRU J^{NE} 15· 5A" (at the nape of the neck). Mannequin doll, movable head of bisque, blue paperweight eyes, closed mouth, real hair wig, mannequin body made of wood, wooden hands with jointed fingers (see illustration on pages 30 and 31), 40in (102cm), circa 1890.

Chapter 2

Bru Surprise Doll

In 1867 Leon Casimir Bru registered his patent for the *Poupée Surprise*, the so-called surprise or two-faced doll. The one side of the head showed a laughing and the other side a crying face. The head was rotated manually and thus the wanted element of surprise was created, without the wig of the doll having to be moved. The technically simple (see patent drawing on page 9), but effective toy was at that time very much loved, but the Bru collectors of today are astounded by the fact that such a toy had been produced by the House of Bru, which had become respected for their other achievements. The same is to be noticed for the earlier doll with a crying mechanism (see page 8).

Leon Casimir Bru, Poupée Surprise, the so-called surprise doll. Two-faced reversible head made of bisque, fastened to a wooden pole. One face laughs and the other cries. Painted blue eyes, open-closed mouth with painted teeth, crossed arms made of bisque, original clothing, 15½in (39cm), circa 1870.

Chapter 3

Bru Bébé Breveté

Leon Casimir Bru, Bru Breveté. Socket head on breastplate made of bisque, leather body with forearms and hands made of bisque, 19½in (50cm), circa 1880.

The head of the Bébé Breveté, apart from having a size number, is unmarked; the same with the breastplate. It has a lovely round childlike face with an inclination towards a double chin and has hardly any similarities of the "Bru familiarity," because this doll belongs to the earlier period. The coloring is delicate.

The body of the Bébé Breveté is seen very clearly to be a model of the lady doll body made of leather. The pattern is similar but the proportions are far more childlike (1:5). New are the forearms made of bisque; they are similar to that of the Gesland Bébés with the Gaultier head. This is a further identification that this company was the possible producer of bisque parts for Bru at that time. The sticker on the breast of this doll is oval in shape with the following inscription: "BÉBÉ BREVETÉ S.G.D.G. PARIS." Naturally, this label may be missing. However, this body is very typical and can be easily recognized without it.

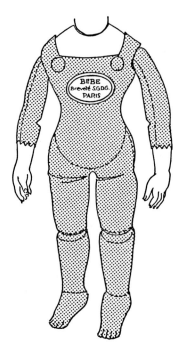

The body of the Bébé Breveté
is nearly complete made of leather,
with forearms made of bisque.

Leon Casimir Bru, Bru Breveté, unmarked socket head on breastplate made of very light bisque, 11in (28cm), circa 1880.

Page 37: Leon Casimir Bru, Bru Breveté, marked "2/0" (on the neck). Socket head on a breastplate made of bisque, blue paperweight eyes, closed mouth, leather body with forearms and hands made of bisque, 15-1/2in (39cm), circa 1880.

Bru Bébé Breveté.

Bru Bébé Breveté.

Above and page 41: Leon Casimir Bru, Bru Breveté marked "2/0" (on the back of the head). Socket head on a breastplate made of bisque, blue paperweight eyes, open-closed mouth, childlike leather body with forearms and hands made of bisque, old clothing, 14in (36cm), circa 1879.

Chapter 4

Circle Dot Bru

*Leon Casimir Bru marked with dot in a circle. Socket head
on a breastplate made of bisque, original mohair wig,
blue paperweight eyes, heavy childlike leather body with
forearms made of bisque, 30in (76cm), circa 1885.*

In 1879 the Bébé Bru experienced several major changes. The head, to be precise the face, was totally remodeled. The face had become far more childlike with chubby cheeks and lips, a slightly opened mouth, found quite often with a molded tongue or an indication of teeth. It is a perfect portrait of a well-nourished small child with milk teeth. This type of head was used over a period of several years, even as the BRU J^NE head was created. That is why it can still be found on the Chevrot body, especially with dark colored dolls, since the full lower lip was very suitable for a black doll.

The markings of this doll can be found on the back of the head, on the breastplate and sometimes on the top of the forehead and may be different. Essentially, one will find a circle and dot and that is why it is called as such. Several of the markings are shown below. The leather body, as well as the breastplate, were altered. The breastplate received molded breasts with pink-tinted nipples, a further attribute of a well-nourished child. To emphasize these breasts, the framing of the breastplate with leather was disposed of. The body was newly tailored (eight parts), chubbier and, therefore, more childlike; the waist disappeared. Also, the body was stuffed with lighter filling material, for example, horsehair, oats or cork shavings and, therefore, it was easier for children's hands to handle. The Circle Dot Bru, more often than not, took up a permanent sitting position because the stuffing blocked up the seams. This small blemish is put up with by Circle Dot admirers.

Head	Forehead	Breastplate
⊙; ⌒; ◉;	B	8
⊙ BRU·J^NE 13	B^te S.G.D.G.	DEPOSÉ
◠	BRU S.G.D.G.	BRU J^NE N°7

Above and page 45: Leon Casimir Bru. Markings found on neck: circle, dot and crescent.
Forehead marked "B^{te} SGDG BRU." Socket head on a breastplate made of bisque,
blue paperweight eyes, original blonde mohair wig, open-closed mouth with molded and
painted teeth, childlike leather body, forearms and hands made of bisque, original clothing,
approximately 17in (44cm), circa 1880.

Above and page 47: Leon Casimir Bru. Markings on neck: circle, dot and crescent. Forehead marked "B^{te} SGDG BRU." Above: Girl with black wig and wearing a low-necked dress. Page 47: Young boy with an original blonde mohair wig, socket head on a breastplate made of bisque, brown paperweight eyes, open-closed mouth with molded and painted teeth, childlike leather body, forearms and hands made of bisque, old clothing, approximately 17in (44cm), circa 1880.

Leon Casimir Bru marked with a circle, dot and crescent. Socket head on a breastplate made of bisque, brown paperweight eyes, open-closed mouth with painted teeth, childlike leather body, forearms and hands made of bisque, 23in (58cm), circa 1880.

Opposite page: Leon Casimir Bru marked with a dot in a circle. Socket head on breastplate made of bisque, dark brown paperweight eyes, open-closed mouth with painted teeth, childlike leather body, forearms and hands made of bisque, 19in (48cm), circa 1885.

*Leon Casimir Bru marked with a circle and dot. Socket head on a breastplate made of bisque,
blue paperweight eyes, open-closed mouth, blonde mohair wig, slim leather body with forearms
and hands made of bisque, 8¹/₂in (22cm), circa 1885.*

*Opposite page: Leon Casimir Bru marked with a circle, dot and crescent. Socket head on a
breastplate made of bisque, mohair wig, open-closed mouth with painted teeth, brown paperweight
eyes, childlike leather body with forearms and hands made of bisque, 24¹/₂in (62cm), circa 1880.*

Leon Casimir Bru, a brown Bru, marked with a dot in a circle. Socket head on a breastplate made of bisque, dark brown paperweight eyes, open-closed mouth, leather body with forearms and hands made of bisque, 14in (36cm), circa 1885.

Opposite page: Leon Casimir Bru, a brown Bru, marked with a dot in a circle. Shoulder head on a breastplate made of bisque, dark brown paperweight eyes, open-closed mouth with painted teeth, childlike kid leather body with forearms and hands made of brown bisque, 16½in (42cm), circa 1885.

Chapter 5

Bru Bébé Téteur
Bru Bébé Gourmand

Leon Casimir Bru Bébé Téteur marked "BRU J^NE O." Socket head on a breastplate made of bisque, brown paperweight eyes, open mouth, original mohair wig, butterfly screw on the nape of the neck, leather body with forearms and hands made of bisque, original clothing and pillow, 12in (30cm), circa 1883.

Both bébés have a slightly altered Circle Dot head. For both of these the mouth had to be opened, a round opening, which was able to fit around the dummy of a baby bottle or in the case of the Bébé le Gourmand, food particles. This so-called "Hole in the Face" is in an aesthetic way rather disturbing, but this impression is slightly softened because the Bébé le Gourmand has a movable tongue, which in the normal case fills out this hole. Quite often this tongue no longer exists. In such a case, this head is then similar to that of the Bébé le Téteur.

The Bébé le Téteur head is found on different types of bodies, such as on the earlier Circle Dot body, the Chevrot body, on a wooden or composition body or even on a S.F.B.J.-Jumeau body. The Bébé le Gourmand had always, due to technical reasons, a Circle Dot body with bisque legs, which had an opening on the soles of the feet so that the food could easily be removed. These legs are very detailed and realistically formed, which took away some of the heaviness of the circle dot body. The markings below are the ones used for the Bébé le Téteur, except for the right-hand marking, a half-moon and crescent, which was used for the Bébé le Gourmand.

⊙
BRU. J.ᴺᴱ   BRU. J.ᴺᴱ   BRU J.ᴺᴱ   DEPOSÉ
9   5T   4   T   ◠

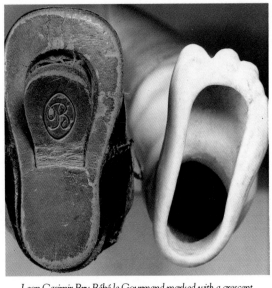

Leon Casimir Bru Bébé le Gourmand marked with a crescent and dot. Body marked "BÉBÉ BREVETÉ S.G.D.G." Socket head on a breastplate made of bisque, blue paperweight eyes, open mouth, childlike leather body with forearms and hands, as well as lower legs and feet made of bisque, opening in the foot and shoe sole so that food can be removed, 18½in (47cm), circa 1883.

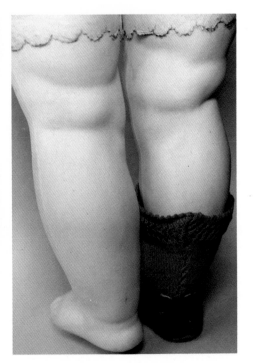

Above and page 57: Leon Casimir Bru Bébé Téteur marked "BRU J^NE 4." Socket head on a wooden body, blue paperweight eyes, open mouth, original mohair wig, 12½in (32cm), circa 1885. The butterfly screw on the nape of the neck is clearly visible. A rubber container for fluids is located inside of the head.

Leon Casimir Bru marked "BRU." Socket head on a breastplate made of bisque, blue paperweight eyes, mohair wig, open mouth, leather body, an old dress, 12½in (32cm), circa 1880.

Page 59: Leon Casimir Bru Bébé Téteur marked "BRU J^{NE} 5 T." Socket head on a breastplate, open mouth, brown paperweight eyes, original wig, leather body with forearms and hands made of bisque, old clothing, 16½in (42cm), circa 1885.

Chapter 6

Bru Jne
Bru Jne R

Leon Casimir Bru marked "BRU J^{ne} 8." Socket head on a breastplate made of bisque, brown paperweight eyes, open-closed mouth, Chevrot leather body with forearms and hands made of bisque, lower legs and feet made of wood, 24-1/2in (63cm), circa 1885.

The improved, more mobile leather body of the Chevrot Bru (Patent: November 23, 1883) has already been described in detail and the inside of the body is described in the patent drawing. However, it is very interesting to note that apart from arms being made out of bisque, arms of wood were also made. These were not wooden copies of the bisque made "ballerina hands," but on the contrary, the hands were angled outwards, like with the hands from other composition bodies. The forearms made of wood do not have any wrist joints and are later found also in this form on the jointed Bru body.

The head, which usually is combined with this new body, is found quite frequently and is popular among collectors, is marked "BRU J^{NE}." It has a face of an older child with characteristic features and does not have such chubby cheeks, but nevertheless it has a soft girlish expression. Sometimes the Circle Dot head or that of the Bébé le Téteur is also found on this body. The markings on the head and breastplate are quite uniform.

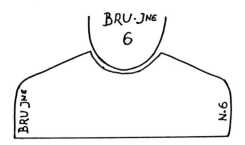

The breastplate is marked likewise, left "BRU J^{NE}" and on the right the size number. Moreover, the head and shoulder number should correspond. However, Bru did not always keep to this rule and, therefore, unfavourable proportions occurred (dolls with a "water head," or with a too heavy body). In the ideal case, it should look like this:

The breastplate and body are connected with a serrated edge (notched) leather band, with larger dolls, two leather bands. The famous paper sticker was glued onto this band and if copied by imitators, they were then threatened with legal action. The paper sticker looked like this:

BÉBÉ BRU B^{TÉ} S.G.D.G.
Tout Contrefacteur sera saisi et poursuivi
Conformément á la Loi

Above and on page 63: Leon Casimir Bru marked "BRU J^{NE} 7." Socket head on a breastplate, both made of bisque, dark brown paperweight eyes, closed mouth, original dark blonde real hair wig, Chevrot leather body with forearms and hands made of bisque, lower legs and feet made of wood, 17½in (45cm), circa 1885.

Above: Leon Casimir Bru marked "BRU J^{NE} 8," circa 1883.

Page 65: Leon Casimir Bru marked "BRU J^{NE} 8." Socket head on a breastplate made of bisque, blue paperweight eyes, closed mouth, leather body, forearms and hands made of bisque, wooden lower legs and feet, 23¹/₂in (60cm), circa 1885.

Above: Leon Casimir Bru marked "BRU J^{NE} 5." Socket head on breastplate made of bisque, open-closed mouth, blue paperweight eyes, original wig, leather body with forearms and hands made of bisque, wooden lower legs and feet, 17in (43cm), circa 1885.

Page 67: Leon Casimir Bru marked "BRU J^{NE} 6." Socket head made of bisque, brown paperweight eyes, open-closed mouth, original blonde fur wig, wooden body with 12 joints, wooden hands, 13½in (35cm), circa 1885.

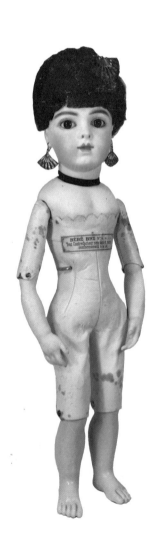

Leon Casimir Bru marked "BRU J^{NE} 7." A so-called Oriental Bru, socket head on breastplate made of bisque, dark brown paperweight eyes, open-closed mouth, original mohair wig, fan-shaped earrings with matching hair clip, Chevrot leather body (see left), original silk kimono with hand-embroidery, 18in (46cm), circa 1885.

Above and page 71: Leon Casimir Bru marked "BRU J^{ne} 11." Socket head made of bisque, blue paperweight eyes, open-closed mouth, real hair wig, composition wooden body with voice box (see above), 25in (64cm), circa 1889.

Leon Casimir Bru marked "BRU J^{NE} 6." Socket head on breastplate made of bisque, brown paperweight eyes, original mohair wig, open-closed mouth, Chevrot leather body with forearms and hands made of bisque, lower legs and feet made of wood, original blue dress with lace trimmings, 19in (48cm), circa 1885.

*"How would you like to see me?", asks the small Bru, and shows herself from the best side of
her changeable personality. It is left to the observer to choose her favorite expression:
questioning, astounded, saucy or prudent.*

Leon Casimir Bru marked on neck "BRU J^{ne} 10;" marked on back of breastplate "BRU J^{ne}
N.O." Socket head on breastplate made of bisque, blue paperweight eyes, open-closed mouth,
Chevrot leather body with forearms and hands made of bisque, carved wooden feet,
26-1/4in (67cm), circa 1885.

Page 75: Leon Casimir Bru marked "BRU J^{ne} 10." Socket head on breastplate made of bisque,
blue paperweight eyes, open-closed mouth, Chevrot leather body with forearms and hands made
of bisque, lower legs and feet carved from wood, 26-3/4in (68cm), circa 1885.

Above and page 77: Leon Casimir Bru marked "BRU J^{ne} 9." Socket head made of bisque, dark brown paperweight eyes, closed mouth, old real hair wig, wooden body with 12 joints with pegs (without rubber bands), 24-1/2in (62cm), circa 1880.

Motion study of the doll described on page 76, "BRU J^{ne} 9."
It demonstrates the flexibility of its wonderful jointed body.

Above and page 81: Leon Casimir Bru marked "BRU J^{NE} 6." Socket head on breastplate made of bisque, brown paperweight eyes, open-closed mouth, original mohair wig, leather body with forearms and hands made of bisque, 18-1/2in (47cm), circa 1885.

Leon Casimir Bru marked "BRU J^{ne} 6." Socket head on breastplate made of bisque, brown paperweight eyes, open-closed mouth, real hair wig, Chevrot leather body with forearms and hands made of bisque, lower legs and feet made of wood, original clothing made of marine blue velveteen decorated with lace, 18½in (47cm), circa 1886.

Above: Leon Casimir Bru marked "BRU J^{ne} 9." Socket head on breastplate made of bisque, open-closed mouth with molded tongue, brown paperweight eyes, dark blonde real hair wig, Chevrot leather body with forearms and hands made of bisque, lower legs and feet made of wood, 24½in (62cm), circa 1880.

Page 85: Leon Casimir Bru marked "BRU J^{ne} 5." Socket head on breastplate made of bisque, open-closed mouth, brown paperweight eyes, original mohair wig, leather body with forearms and hands made of bisque, lower legs and feet made of wood, 19in (48cm), circa 1885.

Above and page 87: Leon Casimir Bru marked "BRU J^{ne} 2." Socket head on breastplate made of bisque, stationary brown paperweight eyes, open-closed mouth, mohair wig, leather body, forearms and hands made of bisque, lower legs and feet made of wood, 13½in (34cm), circa 1885.

Leon Casimir Bru marked "BRU J^{ne} 9." Socket head on breastplate made of bisque, open-closed mouth, mohair wig, Chevrot leather body, forearms and hands made of bisque, lower legs made of wood, old clothing from that period, 23½in (60cm), circa 1885.

Leon Casimir Bru marked "BRU J^{NE} 4." Socket head on breastplate made of bisque, blue eyes, closed mouth, original mohair wig, Chevrot leather body with forearms and hands made of bisque, lower legs and feet made of wood, 16½in (42cm), circa 1887.

Leon Casimir Bru marked "BRU J^{ne} 11." Socket head on breastplate made of bisque, light blue paperweight eyes, open-closed mouth, mohair wig, Chevrot leather body with forearms and hands made of bisque, lower legs and feet made of wood, 28¼in (72cm), circa 1884.

Above and page 93: Leon Casimir Bru mechanical walking doll marked "BRU J^{ne} R 11."
Socket head made of bisque, light blue paperweight eyes, closed mouth, real hair wig, composition
body with built-in walking mechanism, forearms and hands made of bisque, original clothing,
24¼in (62cm), circa 1891.

Leon Casimir Bru marked "BRU J^{ne} R 8 Y.M." Socket head made of bisque, brown paperweight eyes, closed mouth, composition body with eight joints, 19¾in (50cm), circa 1890.

Leon Casimir Bru & Cie marked "BRU J^{ne} R 12." Socket head made of bisque, brown glass sleep eyes, open mouth with four upper teeth, mohair wig, composition body with ten joints, 27½in (70cm), circa 1890.

Leon Casimir Bru marked "BRU J^{ne} 14." Socket head made of bisque, blue paperweight eyes, closed mouth, blonde mohair wig, wooden composition body with voice box, 30¼in (77cm), circa 1888.

Leon Casimir Bru marked "BRU J^{ne} 5." Socket head, open-closed mouth, brown paperweight eyes, original mohair wig, leather body, 18⅞in (48cm), circa 1885, (also see page 85).

Leon Casimir Bru marked "BRU J^{ne} 14." Socket head made of bisque, blue paperweight eyes, open-closed mouth, original real hair wig, wooden body with 10 joints, 31½in (80cm), circa 1890.

A group of charming lady dolls from the Doll Museum, Stein am Rhein, four Bru Bébés and a Petite Dumontier (in the violet dress).

Page 97: Leon Casimir Bru marked "BRU J^{ne} 8." Socket head made of bisque, brown paperweight eyes, closed mouth, composition body with eight joints, 18½in (47cm), circa 1890.

Bru Dolls Made from Gutta Percha

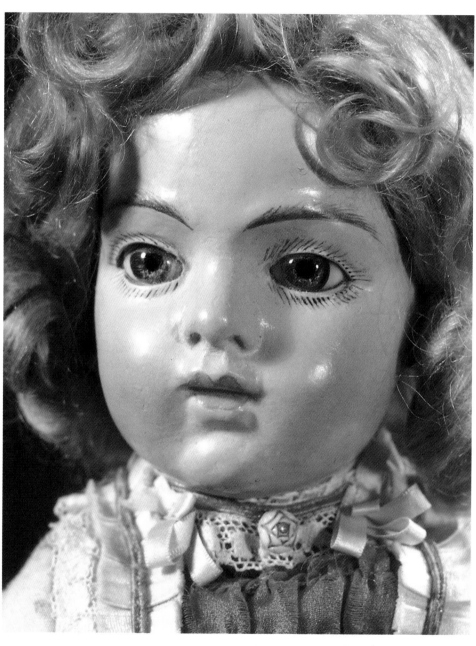

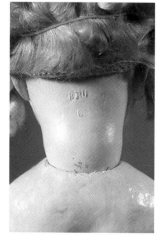

Leon Casimir Bru marked "BRU C" (or BRU 6). Socket head made of Gutta Percha, blue paperweight eyes, closed mouth, composition body with ten joints, unmarked body, Some restoration, Appropriately redressed, 16⁷/₈in (43cm), circa 1890, a very rare doll. Zelda H. Cushner Collection. Photographs by Richard Merrill.

Anatomical Details

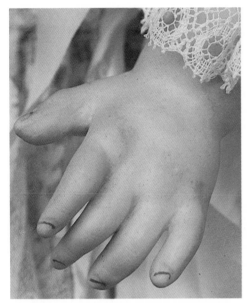

A realistic anatomically-shaped hand of a Circle Dot Bru.

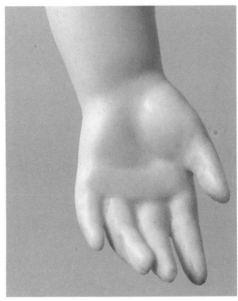

Palm with fingers spread apart, a BRU J^{ne}.

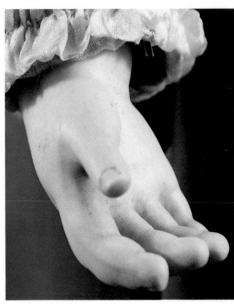

A wonderfully modeled hand of a BRU J^{ne} (page 92).

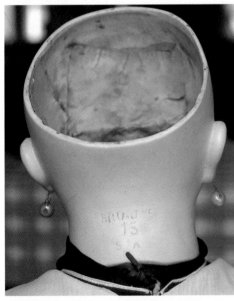

This photograph shows how thin the porcelain is and the very clear marking.

The head opening covered with a cork pate and the markings of a Circle Dot Bru.

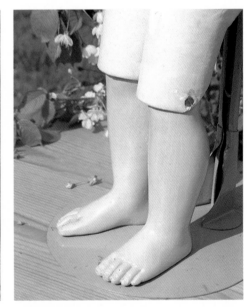

Carved wooden feet of a BRU J^{ne}, with the well-modeled slim toes.

A close-up shows how correctly the face of BRU J^{ne} was painted.

The love of detail is shown here between the connection of the breastplate to the leather body of a Bébé Bru.

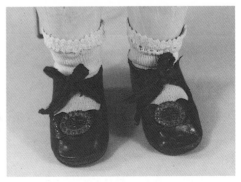

All Bru dolls were dressed well. Here you can see the fine detailed leather shoes.

Reproductions — Fakes

Reproduction of a so-called Chevrot Bru from Elke Schuldt.

The continuous increase in prices of French dolls, especially with Bru dolls, has caused reproductions of old dolls to take a non-underestimatable place in the doll world. Let us put aside the phenomenon of doll reproductions as a hobby. An attentive visitor at doll fairs cannot avoid seeing that several professional producers of reproductions have in the meantime reached an astounding proficiency. There are examples which can withstand any critical eye.

The following logical question arises about this subject: How can one recognize a fake? The answer, however, is not very simple and it requires the training of the mind and eye of the collector. In general, such reproductions are always marked as such by the producers; namely, the mark is deeply imprinted into the bisque so that it cannot be easily removed; but let us make an example, for instance, what happens if someone intentionally has "forgotten" to do this, and someone else tries to sell a doll made in 1985 as a doll made in 1885. What does one look out for?

First look at the painting. The largest problem of reproducing the head is in painting in the typical style of the company. Why is this? If one can imagine, a worker of that period painted day-in and day-out nothing but eyelashes and eyebrows. It will become clear to us that in time a certain confidence and easiness was attained in the paint stroke, whereas today, even with a lot of practice and a talent in painting, this proficiency is never reached. Now have a look through your doll books. Try to pick out the typical pecularities of the style of painting from each individual company. Bru has a totally different style to that of Steiner and Jumeau. Earlier dolls were painted paler as compared to the later dolls. The eyebrows of an earlier Bru are completely different to those of a later Girard Bru. Try to observe and compare these old dolls. Especially with Bru, the very good reproductions are often "too beautiful to be true." A second helpful characteristic: check the porcelain. A lot of reproductions are made of a pink-toned porcelain. The inside of the head will also be pink. However, even if white porcelain was used and the complexion was very well achieved, the porcelain itself will feel totally different, namely smooth and "soapy." Even if a very skilled "artist" was able to copy the surface structure of old

Reproduction of a BRU J^ne from Elke Schuldt. Socket head on breastplate made of bisque; new; very striking light blue paperweight eyes.

bisque, the production technique of the head would give him away. Bru heads were, apart from very later models, not poured, but were pressed into shape with porcelain plates. Due to this, the mold edge fell away and the surface of the bisque inside of the head was as rough as sandpaper. This applies to other dolls of this period, like Jumeau, Steiner, A.T. and so forth. Consequently, try to examine your doll, whenever you have the chance, train your eyes, sense of touch and common sense — or let yourself be advised by specialists. The next time you are at a doll show, try and look far more closely at a reproduction. Only through comparison will you be able to learn the differences.

Reproductions can be recognized at first sight because they have a certain new radiance. Clothes, shoes, wigs and also the body are new. A forger can change all this. He can alter the head artificially using dirt. He can insert old paperweight eyes, use old wigs, cork pates and clothes, but he will always have a problem trying to find a matching old body. With Jumeau it is relatively easy but with Bru and especially with the Chevrot Bru, it is extremely difficult. The body alone costs a small fortune and also French clothing, paperweight eyes and a mohair wig are very expensive. Adding to all this is the investment into a porcelain workshop, as well as the long road to becoming perfect. All these factors together make the reproduction of a French luxury doll a difficult and expensive operation, which would only be worth doing, if one mass-produced these dolls. That this is impossible, is naturally explained by itself.

It is well-known that many collectors have fallen for fakes. However, with more knowledge, this could have been prevented. What is the old saying? One only learns through mistakes! There are also perfect fakes hanging in picture galleries and in some private antique collections one will always find a cuckoo's egg. If it is possible for a forger to overcome all of the above mentioned points and is able to produce a perfect fake doll, which cannot be differenciated from a real one, then this piece of artwork is worth its price.

For comparison, a real BRU J^{ne}. Socket head on breastplate made of bisque, old blue paperweight eyes.

101

A colored fashion print from 1880. The one lady is showing the other lady her elegantly dressed doll which could have been a Bru.

Index

Treasury of German Dolls by *Lydia Richter.* Over 225 color photographs and illustrations plus detailed descriptions of German bisque, parian and china dolls, plus their clothing, hats and accessories are shown. **160 pages. 8¾" x 11⅛". Cloth. Item #4011. $39.95**

Treasury of French Dolls by *Lydia Richter.* Over 100 French bisque, parian and china dolls are beautifully presented, including swivel-head and shoulder-head dolls, portrait, character, reproduction, mechanical and automatic dolls. **144 pages. 8¾" x 11⅛". Cloth. Item #4012. $39.95**

Käthe Kruse — Leben und Werk (Käthe Kruse — Her Life and Work) by *Sabine Reinelt.* The fascinating story of the spirited dollmaker who created some of the most sought-after dolls in the world. German language edition. **186 b/w and 114 color photos. 160 pages. 9¼" x 12¾". Cloth. Item #3792. $39.95**

Charakterpuppen (Puppen Album 4) by *Lydia Richter.* Germany's most delightful character dolls appear in a fascinating photo extravaganza. German language edition. **157 color photos. 128 pages. 9" x 11½". Cloth. Item #3752. $39.95**

Orientalen, Negerpuppen & Exoten (Puppen Album 5) by *Lydia and Joachim Richter.* Unusual and rare oriental, black and exotic dolls presented in a colorful look at these imaginative creations. German language edition. **139 color photos. 128 pages. 9" x 11½". Cloth. Item #3753. $39.95**

Puppenstars (Doll Stars) by *Lydia Richter.* A spectacular color photo album of French and German beauties for anyone who appreciates beautiful dolls. German language edition. **288 color photos. 152 pages. 9" x 11¾". Cloth. Item #3626. $39.95**

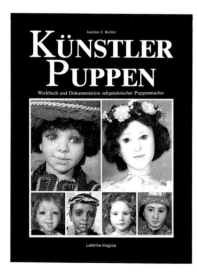

Künstler Puppen (Artist Dolls) by *Joachim Richter.* 32 outstanding contemporary doll artists and their incredibly life-like works are featured in this beautiful color picturebook. German language edition. **270 color photos. 144 pages. 9" x 11¾". Cloth. Item #3627. $39.95.**

Künstler Puppen Two (Artist Dolls Two) by *Joachim Richter.* A second volume of exquisite all new photographs of 49 of the most talented doll artists in the world and their lovely creations. German language edition. **270 color photos. 176 pages. 9" x 11¾". Cloth. Item #3895. $39.95**

Available from
Hobby House Press, Inc.
Cumberland, MD 21502
Phone: (301) 759-3770
FAX: (301) 759-4940